illuminating darkness
the mystic fireflies

Anindita Bose

Ukiyoto Publishing

All global publishing rights are held by

Ukiyoto Publishing

Published in 2024

Content Copyright ©Anindita Bose

ISBN 9789361725777

All rights reserved.

No part of this publication may be reproduced, transmitted, or stored in a retrieval system, in any form by any means, electronic, mechanical, photocopying, recording or otherwise, without the prior permission of the publisher.

The moral rights of the author have been asserted.

This is a work of fiction. Names, characters, businesses, places, events, locales, and incidents are either the products of the author's imagination or used in a fictitious manner. Any resemblance to actual persons, living or dead, or actual events is purely coincidental.

This book is sold subject to the condition that it shall not by way of trade or otherwise, be lent, resold, hired out or otherwise circulated, without the publisher's prior consent, in any form of binding or cover other than that in which it is published.

www.ukiyoto.com

Dedication

heartfelt gratitude to
Ukiyoto for making this project a success
My beloved professor, Sanjukta Dasgupta
Author Ashwani Kumar
Dr. Amit Shankar Saha
Poet Sunil Bhandari
My father, Mr. Sankar Bose
My uncle, Mr. Dipankar Bose
My friends
My students

MUKTI

my Mother was a firefly,
she illuminated me from the darkness

a few words from me...

When I was growing up, no one told me that I would become a writer one day. I was an introverted child, always the silent one. My school teacher used to say good things about me and at the end of the parents-teachers' meeting she used to tell my mother – 'she doesn't speak in class' – and my mother used to smile. I wondered why my mother smiled each time. Today when I am reflecting on that again, I think I understand now – she, my Ma did not know what to say. Perhaps she wished that I would change, but she did not know the way. But her silent wish was granted by the universe. And even though I could not express myself at that time, I started reading books. Then one day, I scribbled; and then one day words danced around me.

I am thankful to the universe that at least both my beloved mothers – my grandmother (amma) & my Ma - could see that I can write and express myself before they left this world for their journeys forward in the realm of life and death.

In this book :

illuminating darkness –
the mystic fireflies

I have captured some words and created multiple mini worlds. If you are reading this book, it means we are meant to be connected for some reasons, even if that is for a brief moment.

"Anindita Bose belongs to that long line of debut poets discovered by Writers Workshop. *I Know the Truth of a Broken Mirror* had impressed me enough with its raw evocations of pain, to decide to publish it. So, it pleases me now to see that she continues her poetic journey with her second book."

Professor Ananda Lal
Kolkata

illuminating darkness

the mystic fireflies

Anindita Bose's second book of poetry is a collection of 35 poems titled - illuminating darkness / the mystic fireflies - are finely crafted poems that fuse sense and sensibility with intensity and insight. The short poems are deeply subjective, braiding together immemorable moments of love, loss, regret, nostalgia and longing. The introspective poems are astonishingly sincere and candid in their expressions of enchantment and disillusionment. The measured use of language, the line breaks, the use of images, metaphors, symbols, open up doors of perception that are profound and reflective, and yet strikingly use mostly monosyllabic and disyllabic signifiers. The poems gesture towards the arrival of the 21st century young woman poets who are able to confidently write about themselves and the environment without any sense of transgression or guilt. Indeed, Indian English poetry, and specifically, Indian English poetry by women poets have traversed an arduous journey since Toru Dutt and Sarojini Naidu wrote their remarkably significant poetry in English, by blending finely sieved elements of ethnicity and culture-specific allusions.

During the colonial period and during the early period of post-colonialism, Indian women poets writing in English had used intensely personal, subjective and confessional modes of creative expression and their rage, protest and dissatisfaction with the patriarchal norms and its implicated gender injustice were overtly strident. As a result, these poems were sometimes starkly candid. The poems often lacked aesthetic distancing, and rarely used skilled ironic and parodic strategies that could generate a willing suspension of disbelief. Whether a dialogic free for all is superior to a monologic representation is a matter of individual response to any text. However, it is noticeable that since the 1990s Indian women poets now write in their own authentic voices of power and have proved that their voices are not merely an echo of British and American poetry- "unafraid, motivated, clear-sighted...they use English with a sense of ease. Their language, style, rhythms and forms are inventive, original and contemporary." The poems of Anindita Bose fall within this category of the new voices of the new Indian poets who are writing in this era of globalization.

The aesthetic nuances of Bose's short lyrics are evocative and descriptive, mixing sense perceptions and the mediation of subjectivities unobtrusively. The short-lyrics are like verse-pictures, sketching with words the empirical observations, redefining the familiar with poetic imagination and the poise of a skilled user of language, ideas and imagination is remarkable -

a full moon night, some

scattered dreams and

my childhood

one leaf of love and a

few clouds passing by…

But the illumination of darkness can be about psychedelic lights and recreational urban night spots too. So, Bose writes,

"I am not a woman or a man,

I am libido, a natural pact

between you and me, an entity

that nurtures reality

you need weed and whiskey to

teleport, while I can transit

through the glasses of drinks

and sprinkle lust on the apples

too…

(I Offer Apples Too…)

The 35 poems in - illuminating darkness / the mystic fireflies, are divided into 7 sections of 5 poems each. The titles of the sections are tenderly romantic such as 'love flows within souls", "dreams float away with wind" and "words that remain forever". The title of the volume enunciates the dispelling of darkness, both from the geographies of the mind and the physical environment. This pledge of irradiation links itself to the Upanishadic pledge "tamaso ma Jyotir gamaya", the perennial journey from darkness to light. The signifier Fireflies in the title as messengers of twinkling ephemeral lights, casts a spell of enchanting allurement as readers are sure to savour and appreciate the gossamer-light poems *by Anindita Bose. The perceptive photographs by Biswajit Mukherjee that follow each of the 35 poems, contribute to the visual attractiveness to this fine book of poems.*

Sanjukta Dasgupta

January 22, 2022

[Dr. Sanjukta Dasgupta, Professor and Former Head, Dept of English and Former Dean, Faculty of Arts, Calcutta University has been the recipient of the Fulbright postdoctoral fellowship and Fulbright Scholar in Residence grant, Australia India Council fellowship, among others. She is the President, Executive Council, of the Intercultural Poetry and Performance Library, ICCR, Kolkata. In 2018, Sahitya Akademi New Delhi nominated her as the Convenor of the English Language Board and member of the General Council]

Anindita's book of poems, unusually called "illuminating darkness / the mystic fireflies", is a tender exploration of the senses. There is a gentleness of thought even in pain and a generosity of heart even in loss.

Anindita's poems progress through the hope and starry-eyed-ness of love and delve slowly, but steadily, into its inevitable reality-checks and pathos. The poet's craving to reach out and touch other lives (as in 'Letter') is suffused with her desire to connect and her elation in connecting. Her inchoate desires spring forth in the title poem ("she heard stories that fireflies/ lighted darkness to hide their/ incomplete dreams."). But love, alas, for her, lingers but never stays. She says "Everything has a meaning / only if broken into pieces of theories and practicals" - and sometimes the pieces show up as fragments of a broken heart.

The book exemplifies a journey, and as it nears its end, the poet says "there was never/ a me/ never a you/ or/ never a we/ only life evolving". At long last, in her heart, there is a recognition and acceptance, that in relationships we are forever a work-in-progress. And, maybe, our lives are so much richer for it.

This is a book to treasure.

Sunil Bhandari

Kolkata 2022

[Sunil Bhandari is a published poet. His podcast 'Uncut Poetry' is in the top 10% of the world's podcasts. His literary newsletter 'The Uncuts' is already a hit!]

Anindita Bose: An Introduction

Percy Bysshe Shelley in his poem "Ode to the West Wind" desires the west wind to carry him like a leaf, a cloud, a wave and then in a moment of poetic dissociation writes the line "I fall upon the thorns of life! I bleed!" Anindita Bose has experienced the thorns of life and hence she bleeds poetry – poetry that is full of hope to be carried away like a leaf, a cloud, a wave. A sensitive soul who attaches herself emotionally with people and that is what births her poetry for poetry is nothing but either a spontaneous overflow of emotions or an escape from it. Emotion is necessary and she has it. Quoting Shelley again, this time from "To a Skylark", we know that "our sweetest songs are those that tell of saddest thought" and yet we wish to soar like the skylark, want to have its unalloyed joy, share its madness. All these you will find in Anindita Bose. Be it as a poet, be it as the co-founder of Rhythm Divine Poets, be it as an editor of EKL Review, be it as a verbal skills trainer, be it as a painter or be it as a friend, a daughter, a sister, she is attached emotionally and has hopes to fly and be the blithe spirit, a skylark. Her poems emanate from nostalgia, memories almost like a fairy tale filled with hope.

She is the firefly who can illuminate darkness.

Dr. Amit Shankar Saha
Poet, Academician & Professor

Contents

love flows within souls…	1
Sweet Nectar	2
Steam	3
Me & You	4
Lovers	5
Two Worlds	6
dreams float away with wind…	7
I Offer Apples Too	8
Letter	9
Universe	10
So many no..s, never...s, do not...s	11
Ah.. Sweet Rosemary	13
Ex-Lover & Beloved	14
light waits in silence...	15
Little Future	16
Beating Hearts	17
The Fireflies Illuminate Darkness	18
Darkness	19
Memories	20
hidden stories are best...	21
A Mistake	22
Fresh Cuts	23
Spaces In Emptiness	24
The Rains Are Coming	25
Fallen Leaves	28
why thoughts linger around...	29
Platonic Love	30
Stories Within	31
Birds	32
Nowhere Shall I…	33
some meetings are never planned…	34

A Story... Somewhere In Hampi	35
Rain Clouds	36
The Boat	37
That Voice	38
Primitive Love	39
words that remain forever...	40
Souls Sailed Across	41
Echoes Of Life	42
A Different Story	43
Essence Of Living	44
The Last Poem	45
About the Author	*46*

love flows within souls…

Sweet Nectar

a drug of the mind, your voice and breath I sink in ecstasy
you say nothing of love yet I drown deep...
let me be free
from those old chains that were nothing
but illusions
you are the truth
an addiction of my heart a pinch of destiny
blended with love-darts...

Steam

music, short story and a cup of you
a full moon night, some scattered dreams and my childhood
one leaf of love and a few clouds passing by
a sip of you brings joy and songs in my heart
and you are far away in some distant land
not tonight perhaps
but we shall taste each other's nectar soon
and write some pages on the star filled night skies

Me & You

when I sit amidst nature my heart beats in rhyme
bells of centuries love
overflow again in mind
the roses and dreams circle around me and all I can imagine is you loving me
...the river has never stopped yet this time it's waiting
for it feels the sea is near, and a home can be built...
other lands are blurring since you have sowed
the love seeds
now days of solitude and peace are blooming in my dreams

Lovers

a room full of sunshine and shadows of rays
silhouettes of lovers
and whispers of love
empty canvasses of
colours and sketches
some words of poetry and faraway mountains...
you shall be always loved by your first lover
in between those raindrops and rainbows of dreams
one day a ship will sail with all your paper boats
and you will stay behind to walk with your soul

Two Worlds

your and my worlds jingle together in sounds of broken shells
wind chimes dance in sweet motions as the breath of land touches them
our feet in salsa tap the floors in some classical era
your and mine waves did flow in some milky ways
as the earth revolves in energies making the starry nights float
you and I merge together like musical notes

dreams float away with wind…

I Offer Apples Too

it's me, the voice that you and they crave to hear on full moon nights
but I keep silent at times to keep my virtue in the
eyes of those who look for flaws in me
I wear white, bars are my favourite weekend haunts and I reach home at dawns,
while dark nights are my love for they never leave me alone
I pour red wine in glasses full of cut apples, ready to be served
you meet me thinking it is your call,
but telepathy works well on dreaming minds
my lips spell cast of passion on your wits and you walk towards a mortal
ordeal...
I am not a woman or a man, I am libido, a natural pact between you and me, an
entity that nurtures reality
you need weed and whiskey to teleport, while I can transit through the glasses of
drinks and sprinkle lust on the apples too
yet when you meet me in crowds, or in moments of your dire need, I laugh and
fade away
for they still worship me as sacred...

Letter

the incomplete letter still remained on the first page of her diary when the thunderstorm broke into the village

she looked at the brown leather covered present from her past, a time that has traveled away in

search of other times

she could never write

beyond a few words of

love since the division of a country

and her memories floated in tiny boats of consciousness in those restless moments of solitude

she had written a letter each time the fragments of lost stories hallucinated her

letters that vanished with dawn and returned each night in hopes of reaching her diary...

and now that the village was on the verge of a flood, she wished she could write some more

she wrapped the diary with some old clothes and put it in an old trunk

and when the water engulfed her village, the locked box traveled in search of a reader...

Universe

flowers bloom

universe breathes

silence walks through music of trees

a mild breeze steals my memories

I play with time and wounds looking for your presence

mother, we share a bond of forever

a kind of love, sweet and rare

you grew with me through years and pains

we became two women characters of father's book

he gave us shade and space to grow

like those wild berries of our orchard

we found no one to replace his shadows

so we stitched his shirts again and again

hoping to fossilize images of happiness

my wings have grown they spread to fly

to explore those stories, you shared with me

but I oscillate between now and then wandering at times in another future

I remain for you

I write songs of our

togetherness and I shall be with you

like you had been with me...

So many no..s, never...s, do not...s

so many questions and restrictions
so many duties and responsibilities
so many reasons to feel broken and lost...
woman, with all these truths in your life... you become more strong
there are men who love, admire and respect you
there are families who care for you
there are husbands who support you
there are reasons to feel proud and alive...
woman, with all these realities in your life... you become more powerful
and with strength and power, you create life on earth
woman, there is nothing that can stop you from choosing your own life
yet you believe in sacrifice, balance and unity...
a life-giver, a protector, a wife, a mother, a daughter, a homemaker, a sister, a creator, and what-not?
woman, you are a pillar to those who believe in you!

*Woman, you are a rainbow across
the clear blue sky unfurling the hues
of love in life
a creation to bloom beautiful dreams
a celebration of Mother Supreme*

Ah.. Sweet Rosemary

she would keep my friend safe she would never know what
storms have blown
sweetness would nurture
him and a man will reform,
for she is rosemary
sunflowers will bloom in
barren hearts and my friend shall see love flowing again aimlessly
my words dance out and
form tiny clouds through
which fly out thousands of
dream birds
children will come and
nourish his garden when he would walk his path
while I shall see her,
leaning on his arms and
singing songs of life
together they stand under
the shining sun, while breeze plays with pink bougainvillea and showers the petals
in my dream...

Ex-Lover & Beloved

Lover:
Forgive me and lead your life
Beloved:
Silent
Lover:
Embrace life, be blessed my love
Beloved:
Silent
Lover:
I shall miss you forever but remain silent
Beloved:
Laughs

light waits in silence...

Little Future

I am yet to feel another pink butterfly, a tiny world coming to meet other worlds

I remain in midst of tales known and unknown while the would-be mother awaits for a reality breathing in her womb

we have spun fairy tales together for our future and then sketched them on the walls of our home

we have touched each other at moments, with hope that the skin would not be a barrier anymore

since we are waiting...

you, in a dark world waiting for light and I in the world of light waiting for love...

Beating Hearts

I never knew it has been always you and deep inside my heart a beating song played one lost tune, which I mistook for the unheard music of Nature

it was you and your essence that stopped me from looking beyond the horizon at other passing clouds

but now is too late to tell you what currents have passed through me when I searched for a living love while I witnessed how you walked those steps of rosy romantic sprees

yet you never betrayed me for it was silence between us that kept our bond alive and we shall cherish each other in an eternal bliss

The Fireflies Illuminate Darkness

*the fireflies danced once
more and circled around
unseen dreams
the darkness melted into
tiny dots of flying lights
she sat on the windowsill of
the hotel in the hill station,
looking at those bright hopes
but this time she felt nothing
since she has learnt to love
herself by now...
the blisters caused by some
butts of burning cigarettes do
not haunt her anymore
she heard stories that fireflies,
lighted darkness to hide their
incomplete dreams
a myth or a truth - that a firefly
waits for its eternal love and
sometimes it remains behind to
witness the happiness of its lover
in human form
she silently nurtures the darkness,
secretly waiting for her firefly...*

Darkness

dark dreams
engulf me
I look for a pillar
... you disappear
will you hear me
again
for once at all
while I fly in darkness to unknown alleys
I call you today
I called you yesterday I shall call you tomorrow.
Will you hear...?

Memories

I cannot walk through the rain anymore, or perhaps I can…
I cannot say.
It has been ages since I have felt those drops on my face.
Do you ever feel magical when it drizzles and after a while your hairs write a different story?
I remember…
I think I remember that day.
The first time I realized what rain is… I am not sure if it was the first time. But right now, I see myself on the terrace of my old home.
The first shower after a long,
humid summer.
My feet are running in collected rainwater on the terrace.
It was a game my mother used to play with my father.
The water was never clean.
But we loved those mornings and afternoons, but not the nights.
I was always afraid of thunderstorms. I still am. Perhaps I will always be…
It is strange how we leave behind parts of our lives and go back to them at times.
I miss my old home. I grew up in it.
And now I am another person.
A traveler in a book of my life.

hidden stories are best...

A Mistake

a lemon sized ball, hard with tissues and blood clots

pushing through a hole to escape the death already destined since the word conceive was uttered

it was not yet forty-nine days

nothing would feel the pain, the right time to execute a lifeline like it never was born

soft reddish-brown tissues, warm in the fingers of the untimely motherhood, a steel faucet and cold running water

mimicking pain and nausea, headspins and medicines

used to create a moment of death delivery, the bleeding would continue till the body can hold no more the

reminiscence of tiny muscles

and then everything will be fine. A success. A new day. A return to the old self.

Fresh Cuts

words cut through the body as the lover whispers how many women have brushed his body with fingers, eyes, tongues and genitals

happens, quite a normal fact since humans are natural and polygamy is a tested process

yet words cut through the body as the lover whispers of love and touches the private parts with lust

in the darkest corner of night, the body shivers and repeats the words to examine the weight of attraction for even though those words cut the body, it cannot leave and vanish

the body waits for the sun to come, another day will heal the old cuts and bring the fresh ones ...

Spaces In Emptiness

darkness is not an empty
space, it has a light hidden somewhere deep within
blankness is not an end,
it has motions of memories
buried in apparently calm
mind
emotions are nothing but
illusions dancing as ripples of happiness and sorrows
everything has a meaning
only if broken into pieces of theories and practicals
nothing seems to be true
yet the stream of
consciousness plays an
eternal role
images of dreams and
realities flow
while some of us boxed
in elapse of time, think and wonder what are days and
nights
in midst of stars and falling leaves, some of us welcome both autumns and springs
the roots of trees retell the
stories that cycles begin and complete in series

The Rains Are Coming

to wash away the heat of
all those dreams that float
like clouds in the minds of
millions tired humans, who
wander around in vain to
find the ways that will take
them to the core of this
universe.
For that is found deep within. The rains are coming
to keep away the meaningless
words that haunt the hearts
of people who walk miles each day to discover routes, which
might dissolve their miseries
and fears of existence.
For that is an illusion not to be nurtured.
The rains are coming
to make us understand that
breathing is not an exercise
but the truth that we are alive
to feel and survive, even when the earth needs to be renewed without human intervention.
For sometimes we forget to show gratitude.
The rains are coming
to clean me of my actions that could have been avoided only if I had not been silently following the norms of society, but acting on my own instincts and for the commune responsibilities.

For the micro and the macro are always connected.
The rains are coming

for the souls to pour out the tears that had witnessed the centuries old cycles of death and birth

for everything circles around a reason and nothing can bypass the touch of nature.

The rains are coming

wait at your windows, open your hearts and witness the unfolding of a newness, which will wrap you and inject an eternal blissful energy in your veins that will guide you through your own vertical rise. For resurrection is a dimension that can be reached at will.

Fallen Leaves

the empty swing did swing when I whispered the words of love
I walk alone since the fallen leaves keep repeating their stories to me
the orange sun once visited my loneliness, to extend the heat that keeps nature warm
did you meet those hearts who had left your door since you wanted to explore more
the birds sing songs of a new day that will nurture togetherness
invisible footsteps of lovers from corners of the world walk in search of eternal space
do you weave tales of realities that others believe to be true and live through them...
I sit in silence and observe
the rains fall, the streets get ready for canvases, the dreams begin to float
and a line of tiny red ants move quickly to load food into their holes for the summer will not last forever

why thoughts linger around...

Platonic Love

a new air touched the shore his boat anchored at a corner while his lips let out old smoke

a distant shadow of golden sun and beauty in his loving arms while a storm brew at horizon

engulfed in silence he lit another cigarette and smiled while his presence flickered

at dawn innocence walked by whom his eyes followed till dusk while his imagination trampled it

a butterfly touched his bare shoulders and tears flooded the sea while he walked into the waves

platonic love crisscrossed with desires running deep in minds while he met another story...

Stories Within

he comes like a mild wind and spreads his arms
he says nothing but his pains colour the sky
he looks deep inside her eyes and tells her stories
that he witnessed with others in months of springs
she knows and she feels while thoughts surround her
while he wonders whether he should let go of his past
a moment connects them on a road where souls meet to depart
and he utters words, which scatter her thoughts
and then the road waits for another trip...

Birds

wings spread across the clouds on sunny days
welcoming rain in circles and arrows
the birds on her canvas fly in directions unknown
yet these tiny souls come each day to meet and sing
songs of ancient lives that they have shared with her
a connection somewhere left behind in layers of life
coloured with each cycle of birth and death
fading like dust in memories only to return at intervals
in blinks of dreams to paint that yesterday, today and tomorrow breathe together

Nowhere Shall I…

nowhere shall I burn
my soul if not in your heart
nowhere shall I rest in peace if not in your home
nowhere shall I explore life if not in your presence
nowhere shall I run to hide if not in your thoughts
nowhere shall I free myself if not in your arms
nowhere shall I meet destiny if not in your dreams
nowhere shall I paint a life if not in your eyes
and now that you are silently listening to my song, I shall catch rainbows and butterflies with my charms…

some meetings are never planned…

A Story… Somewhere In Hampi

I died that moment, in which
you had listened to me and
walked bare chest in front of
those white women
you would say that I was the
reason and you had to listen
since you always do
a ride amidst those bare
mountains on a summer day
and my scarf hiding tears
since the sky knew that your
heart had several thoughts
buried
a village, a hammock, a night,
and a game of chess in dark
shades
the world rolled by, leaving
behind me alone with a few
words that have kept me alive
till today
you would never know, and
never hear about the days of
rains
for you I have crafted
canvases of happy hours

Rain Clouds

a tree wrapped in lights on a deserted night street, an hour or two before feet did walk and cars rushed

time stopped the movement till another day, someone someday invented a day and a night

and since then, the axis has been rotating

two forces work in a society, one does and the other

follows but in scriptures of contemporary collective consciousness has evolved a new fate

a rare group which wants change, even if that means uprooting the age-old beliefs

no fears, no teachings, no walking away from humanity

a parallel cloud fluffing slowly to shower rain soon

The Boat

*enough, has the boat waited for a traveller to take it... far and wide
it has remained tied up to the shore since forever, in search of an adventurer
the thunder had laughed in the past, now gave up
the rainbows allured and then left for those who would
listen
the boat was not taught how to be with other ships, yet once it did try
and what floated behind was skeletons of wood and steel in crystal blue water...
the boat learned to float,
drown and float back to its own parallel shores
and five minutes back it
began a journey across the ocean*

That Voice

I hear a song,
it comes from a faraway land
the voice is not clear
but it makes me travel deep inside my terrain,
in search of my old self, who knew how to survive
amidst the chaotic instincts of rapid changes in human life...
I hear an unknown voice, and it reminds me of my mother, who silently watched the sunshine on afternoons
I remember
I remember many images of my childhood...
were they dreams or reality were they imagination or truth were they mine or life's
were they random or scripted
I want to sit and meditate, but humans cannot when they hear that voice calling them from somewhere deep within...
either it exists or wants to exist.

Primitive Love

*The most primitive love that I shared, is with my grandmother
we walked through my innocence, while exploring my experience
she taught me about life, yet kept me in dark about the darkness of this world...
I learnt about the universe, but I did not know that dreams break
and we scatter like molecules.
Perhaps she wanted me to be happy, all through my life, as long as I could...
since that keep us fresh like newly bloomed flowers.
She knew, she faced, she experienced...
and she wanted me to know, to face, and to experience... slow, real slow.*

words that remain forever...

Souls Sailed Across

Yesterday some souls sailed across a water path
the rain did not come, yet
hearts poured
some coins went deep into a land of fishes
where wishes are heard and fulfilled.
Words connect the world and dreams
yet moments revolve as passing shadows
leaving behind traces of those, who knows how to keep footsteps.

Echoes Of Life

a voice that I loved,
a voice that nourished me,
a voice that taught me
to be bold
I haven't heard that voice
for five years...
a void, empty, dark silence.
I sit, and wait for nothing,
since a few years are enough
for life to teach us that no
matter how much we cry, or
shout, or feel hurt -
the loved ones gone, shall
never return.
Now is the time...
to tell them
to love them
to be with them
...there is no tomorrow for love.

(My grandmother was my world, she still is, yet I never recorded her voice. What a mistake I have made...)

A Different Story

I waited long enough
to love my parents
to take care of old age
to know that life is not what we plan
to hear people say that they adore me
to understand life better...
Have you experience enough to reach me
to be the one to tell me a a different story about life?
If you do, reach me, tell me, I might believe you...
But remember, I have seen life, selfless love, peace and death
and so, bring a story that is strongly about life and not some imagination of your mind...

Essence Of Living

I have fears...

just like you.

I could not walk many times towards the places where I should have been at that right time...

that doesn't mean I did not care.

I wanted to,

but I was scared to reach choices that could have

made me leave behind the memories...

I could not fly many times, yet I made my way through the sky

the silence that I held in my core, taught me the secrets of living a life without wishes of ignoring death

and so, I know, that I will meet every essence of living life itself...

The Last Poem

through senses the sun rises
my last breath and years of life have given me a peaceful truth
there was never
a me
... never a you
or
never a we
only life evolving

About the Author

Anindita Bose

Anindita Bose was born in Calcutta. She has two poetry books and one short story collection, which are widely acclaimed; she is an independent script-writer, subtitles-writer, translator of several Bengali books and poems. She is an academician, and is the co-founder of Rhythm-Divine-Poets, editor of EKL-Review, program manager of Chair Poetry Evenings, Kolkata's International-Poetry-Festival. She mentors people for Study Abroad Programs. She was invited and felicitated in 2023 by - Bangla Akademi at Kobita Utsav, Kolkata and UDAYGIRI foundation, Bhubaneswar.